God's Delight

a book of verse for children

Catherine Valentine

Illustrations by
Jessica Holly

Dedicated to all the children of T. Allen and Jamey Burr.

Thank you to the friends and family who generously donated to make this book a reality.

MR. SQUIRREL IN THE RAIN

Mr. Squirrel darts in the rain
he runs this way and that way.
He chatters on, sharing news
with the birds and bugs.
Twitching tail always moving,
he forgets sometimes
to stop and enjoy a nut.
But when he does,
he is filled with delight
and the world stops.
He munches and chomps,
his head filled with happy thoughts.

CREATION
(Published in Pure in Heart Stories Issue #8)

How the old oak delights me!
Rough is your covering, strong and sure.
My Father sent the wind through your leaves.

How I'm enchanted by the butterfly!
Beauty in delicacy, soft and fluttering.
My Father painted your wings.

How the howl of the wolf thrills me!
Powerful and haunting in the deep night.
My Father deemed that you should sing.

How the deer leaps through the grass!
Grace upon grace, eyes always watching.
My Father gave you the wide lands.

How high the eagle flies!
Majestic! You soar over deep waters.
My Father said, "Take the skies!"

How the cougar prowls the land!
Elusive with strength and pride.
My Father gave you shelter in the heights.

How the otter touches my heart!
Friendly and lovable, such comfort.
My Father said, "Go play in the waters."

SPRING—IN LIKE A LAMB

March came in gently,
warm breezes are welcome.
The birds are happy and friendly.
March came in gently—
joyful spirits are in plenty
and sour faces are seldom.
March came in gently,
warm breezes are welcome.

A RAINY DAY

Rain drops drip, drip, drip
on my eyelashes and nose.
My feet go splish splash.

BIRD

A bird flies into the sky
and I feel much delight.
How it swoops and glides!
A bird flies into the sky
and makes me wish I could fly.
It soars to a great height.
A bird flies into the sky
and I feel much delight.

LOST SHEEP

A frightened sheep among the trees,
how did she end up lost?
Where's her Savior? She's in need!
A frightened sheep among the trees,
but Jesus came! He heard her plea
and she's worth the journey's cost.
A frightened sheep among the trees,
how did she end up lost?

CREATURES

The ant rushes to find food for its kin,

always working, lazy it has never been.

Butterfly flutters around the flower,

so much beauty, no one could be dour.

The spotted fawn asleep in the tall grass,

without worry, the danger will soon pass.

Echoes of coyotes in the deep woods,

their chatter fills the night under the moon.

A bear walks slowly to the rushing creek,

enjoying the quiet life as he drinks.

The robin sings her joyful melodies,

tired souls hear and find such remedy.

EARLY MORNING WALK IN SOUTHERN ILLINOIS

Early morning light

bathes the earth

and beautiful things

greet my eyes.

The burning sun

coming over the horizon,

red clover and daisy fleabane

reaching out to me

as I walk the dusty country road.

I spot Carolina horsenettle

hiding in the ditch, shy little thing.

Wild carrot blooms

looking like old-fashioned lace.

Bird songs are softly heard

and I see them swoop

over the fields of soybeans.

Such delight is a morning walk.

SONG OF CREATION

If you listen closely, you can hear the melody,
the sweet notes on the shoulders of the wind.
The rhythm of the drums between the mountains
and the cymbals among the clouds.
The symphony of creation has begun its song,
with the first signs of spring, it struck the first chord.
But the beauty of the song is not complete
for the choir has not yet begun to sing.
And as the days grow warmer, all wait breathlessly.
Then at last the first flower blooms, the singer begins to sing,
and with a burst of color, the choir takes the stage.
The deep reds blend with the soft whites
as their angelic voices ring from the earth to the sky.
The song of creation is at its height, can you hear it?
It's being sung for you, for me, for all of mankind.

G.O.O.D.N.I.G.H.T.

Go to sleep, sweet child,

Only the moon should be awake.

Off to bed now, child,

Deep sleep will make tomorrow bright.

Night has fallen and all must be in bed.

I will love you, child, always.

Goodnight, and have no fear,

Hear the owl's sweet hoot?

Tonight I kiss your head with a blessing.

THE CAT

Cat flicks her tail,

walks away in annoyance—

her nose in the air.

SUMMER—SING!

The land is alive!
The summer sun gives kisses
as bees dance and buzz.
Oh sing, my soul, with the birds!
Breathe in the scent of summer.

WILD CHILD

She walks barefoot in the grass in summer;
her delight is in the creek that murmurs.
His eyes search the sky for the rising moon,
the stars' enchanting light will be here soon.
She greets the ancient tree as an old friend;
her heart is broken, but bird songs do mend.
His excitement builds during the spring storms.
He is not sad in rain, nor does he mourn.
Such jubilation over the first snow;
she's not afraid, let the winter winds blow.

IMPATIENT LUCY

My dog Lucy
wants to go for a walk.
She wags her tail
by the door
ever hopeful.
I try to explain,
"The sun isn't up yet."
But she whines,
a little upset
that I still sit in my seat.
I have to tell her no.
Lucy sighs and pouts.
She doesn't understand
that "no" sometimes means
"not yet."

VISITOR AT THE RIVER

I looked out over the river
when to my surprise
a midland watersnake
swam nearby.
I never understand
some people's fright,
especially since
when he spotted me
he dropped his fish
in complete surprise!
How rude I was when I intruded,
when he just wanted lunch.
I, too, wouldn't want to be startled
as I ate my fill at the river.

WONDER

Did Jesus feel the wonder

when He looked up at the stars?

Did He have the awe I felt

as I stood outside and saw them twinkling?

In Jesus's walks on this earth,

did He stop and smell the flowers?

All things were made through Him—

did He enjoy His handiwork?

Did a child run up to Him

to give Him a pretty stone

and was He just as delighted?

This earth is full of wonder—

from sunsets to waterfalls,

from marching ants to cricket songs.

Did Jesus feel happy when He saw it all?

I believe He did, but He was most happy

to see the people give their hearts to Him.

HAILSTORM

Roused from a deep sleep,

a thumping on the roof.

Up from my bed I leap—

roused from a deep sleep.

Hail falls as the sky weeps.

The view from my window gives proof.

Roused from a deep sleep,

a thumping on the roof.

HONEYSUCKLE

Little white flowers—

my tongue tastes the sweet nectar.

A bee flies near me.

AUTUMN—FALLING ASLEEP

As the fall winds blow

I stop and breathe deep.

My sweater feels good

on my chilly skin.

The leaves jump and twirl—

I wonder what music they hear.

The world is falling asleep

and it's time to be at peace.

WINTER—BRIGHTEST LIGHT

Upturned faces to the starry sky
Under their soft light we lie

The warmth and glow of a single lamp
The world outside is cold and damp

Twinkling lights on evergreens
Giving hope and peaceful dreams

A dancing flame on cold nights
Filling us with warmth and delight

Silver light from a full moon
Banishing all sadness and gloom

Snow sparkling under street lights
A dreary world now joyful and bright

In Bethlehem, Jesus was born in a stable
The Brightest Light, lying in a humble cradle

MORNING STORM

In the early morning
thunder rolls in the heavens.
Trees sway and bend
as the wind barrels though.
A flash of lightning
as bird feeders
swing on their hooks—
the birds in hiding.
But, maybe not so,
for I hear the song
of one feathered friend.
A brave little soul
who is not afraid of the storm.
His song is sweet,
a cheerful sound.
I hear, too, the crickets.
Completely unbothered,
singing their song
and unafraid.
I am cheered by their music
as I sit in comfort
and let the storm rage.

BLESSING ON THE SON

Run, my boy, be wild and free!

Play music and find joy in reading.

Fix what is broken and find what's been lost.

Your mind and your hands

are wondrous gifts from our Father above.

After a mistake, may you find the courage

to admit and make amends.

Humbleness is your greatest friend.

Run, my boy, be wild and free!

A blessing to all may you be.

BLESSING ON THE DAUGHTER

Run, my girl, be wild and free!

Use your mind and hands

to your utmost ability.

They are gifts from the Father,

use them wisely.

Your beauty is a heart at rest

and knowing love is from God above,

everything else is but less.

Admit a wrong and make amends;

stay humble, it's for the best.

Run, my girl, be wild and free!

A treasure to all may you be.

PRAISE FOR THE CREATOR

I praise You for the creatures in the deep

and I sing to You for the stars in the night.

I lift my hands for the gazelle who leaps—

I praise You for the creatures in the deep.

I dance for the willow tree that weeps

and I laugh with delight in the mountain heights.

I praise You for the creatures in the deep

and I sing to You for the stars in the night.

LET'S LAUGH

What fun are our animal friends!

See how the penguin walks

and how loud the goose squawks?

The platypus tries to be a duck!

Hear the squirrels fight over nuts?

The panda is such a klutz!

In the jungle are dancing birds—

the noise they make can easily be heard!

God loves to laugh so He gave animals

because today may be hard to handle.

www.ingramcontent.com/pod-product-compliance
Lightning Source LLC
Chambersburg PA
CBHW042055050526
44107CB00110B/1183